THE HEAT OF THE DAY

Harold Pinter was born in East London in 1930.
He is married to Antonia Fraser.

Calderdale College Library
Tel: 01422 399350

WITHDRAWN

This book is issued subject to Library regulations, and is due on or before the date marked above.
You may renew books in person or by telephone 3 times only, quoting the number on the book's Library barcode label.
NB Overdue books are charged at 5 pence per item per day.

D0268539

by the same author

Mountain Language

THE HEAT OF THE DAY

Harold Pinter

adapted from the novel
by Elizabeth Bowen

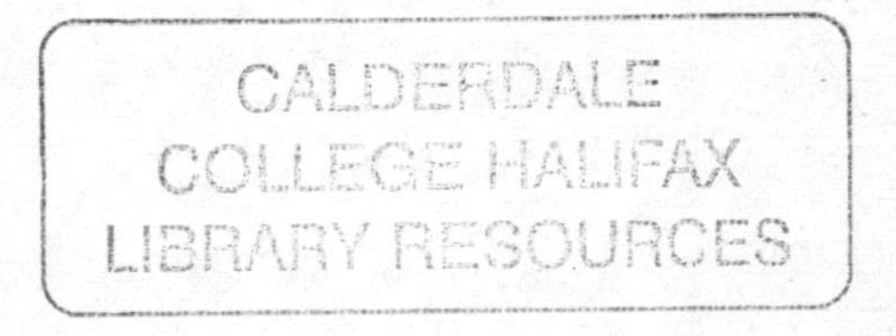

faber and faber
LONDON · BOSTON

First published in 1989
by Faber and Faber Limited
3 Queen Square London WC1N 3AU

Printed in Great Britain by
Richard·Clay Ltd. Bungay, Suffolk

All rights reserved

© Harold Pinter, 1989

This screenplay is based on the novel
The Heat of the Day by Elizabeth Bowen,
published by Jonathan Cape.

Phototypeset by Input Typesetting Ltd, London

This book is sold subject to the condition that it shall not, by way of trade or otherwise, be lent, resold, hired out or otherwise circulated without the publisher's prior consent in any form of binding or cover other than that in which it is published and without a similar condition including this condition being imposed on the subsequent purchaser

British Library Cataloguing in Publication Data is available

ISBN 0–571–14072–6

CALDERDALE
COLLEGE LIBRARY
HALIFAX

DATE 21/10/99
SOURCE David Shaw
CLASS 822 PIN
A/No. 65743
£4.99

COPY No.

The Heat of the Day was produced by Granada Television in 1989. The cast was as follows:

HARRISON	Michael Gambon
STELLA	Patricia Hodge
ROBERT	Michael York
FRANCIS	Ralph Michael
PARLOUR MAID	Tina Earl
MRS TRINGSBY	Hilary Mason
NETTIE	Peggy Ashcroft
DR TRINGSBY	John Gill
TAXI DRIVER	Aubrey Phillips
BLYTHE	Stephen Hancock
LOUIE	Imelda Staunton
RODERICK	Grant Parsons
ERNESTINE	Anna Carteret
MRS KELWAY	Heather Chasen
PETER	Rafael Pauley
ANNE	Jessica Simpson
DONOVAN	David Kelley
HANNAH	Pat O'Toole
MARY	Grace Kinirons

Lighting Cameraman	Jon Woods
Production Designer	Christopher J. Bradshaw
Costume Designer	Jane Robinson
Editor	Andrew Sumner
Music	Ilona Sekacz
Producer	June Wyndham-Davies
Director	Christopher Morahan

J096358

INT. A ROOM. NIGHT

A man sitting at a table. One lamp is lit over the table.
The man is sifting through photographs.
The back of his head. His hands.
The photographs:

ROBERT *in officer's uniform with fellow officers emerging from a London club.*
ROBERT *alone on station platform.*
ROBERT *and* ERNESTINE *at bus stop.*
ROBERT *alone at bus stop.*
ROBERT *and civilian at bus stop.*
Civilian alone at bus stop.
ROBERT *and* STELLA *in Regent's Park, arm in arm.*

Hand puts this photograph aside and continues sifting.

ROBERT *in phone box.*
An empty station platform. Dawn.
A stationary car. Country lane.
ROBERT *and* STELLA *hailing taxi.*
STELLA *in taxi at window.* ROBERT *waving.*

Hand puts these last two aside.

ROBERT *with two men at a street corner. Umbrellas.*
ROBERT *and* STELLA *lying on grass, asleep. She in summer dress. He with open shirt.*
STELLA *lying on the grass. Eyes open.*

Hand puts the first of these two photographs aside, takes single photograph of STELLA *and pins it on to the wall.*

EXT. REGENT'S PARK. SUMMER. DAY

ROBERT *and* STELLA *walking towards trees.*
They pass a man sitting on a bench. It is HARRISON.
ROBERT *and* STELLA *disappear into the trees.*

INT. ROOM

The man at the table stands abruptly. Switches out the light.

EXT. WISTARIA LODGE. MAY. DAY

A taxi arriving.
Cousin FRANCIS *gets out. He wears tweeds. He goes to house, rings brass bell. Silence. Wistaria frames the white pillared porch. The doors open. A* PARLOUR MAID.

PARLOUR MAID
Yes?

FRANCIS
Mrs Tringsby?
In background in the hall a woman speaks.

MRS TRINGSBY
Yes, yes? Oh yes. Do come in. Do come in.
He goes in.

INT. HALL. DAY

FRANCIS
Mrs Tringsby? I'm Francis Morris.
He shakes her hand.

MRS TRINGSBY
Oh dear. Yes, yes. Please, will you come into the drawing room?

FRANCIS
Is my wife in there?

MRS TRINGSBY
No, oh dear no. She likes to be cosy in her room.

FRANCIS

She expects me, I trust?

MRS TRINGSBY *puts her fingers to her lips.*

MRS TRINGSBY

Ssshh. There are other people . . .

She leads him into the drawing room.

INT. DRAWING ROOM. DAY

MRS TRINGSBY *closes the door.*

MRS TRINGSBY

I told her, of course, that you were coming . . . but whether she remembers . . . She loves her wool . . . This is such a quiet house, you see . . . a true home of rest . . . our task is to protect and reassure . . . She loves her wool . . . She's so quiet and content and you haven't of course seen her for . . .

During this she has been staring at him with growing alarm and bewilderment. His eyes are blinking rapidly. He holds on to the table.

. . . and you haven't of course seen her for . . .

He clutches the table, groans, falls, bringing table and vase of flowers over.

MRS TRINGSBY *screams.*

INT. NETTIE'S ROOM. DUSK

NETTIE *sitting with wool. Sound of ambulance arriving.*
NETTIE *continues knitting.*

EXT. WISTARIA LODGE. DUSK

Ambulance men bringing stretcher from the house, body covered in a sheet.

DR TRINGSBY. MRS TRINGSBY *with hands clasped. Faces at the windows. The stretcher is placed in the ambulance.*

Taxi drives into the forecourt and comes to a halt. The DRIVER *looks out of the window. He speaks to* DR TRINGSBY.

DRIVER

Mr Morris?

DR TRINGSBY

What? Who?

DRIVER

Mr Morris. I'm picking him up for the six o'clock train.

DR TRINGSBY

No, no . . . I'm Dr Tringsby.

DRIVER

I brought him here a couple of hours ago.

The ambulance drives off.

DR TRINGSBY

Yes, yes! He's gone away! He's not here!

DRIVER

But he told me to come and pick him up.

DR TRINGSBY

Yes, but he's gone!

DRIVER

But what about my ten bob? He owes me ten bob.

DR TRINGSBY

He's taken it with him!

MRS TRINGSBY *howls, runs into the house.*

INT. COUNTRY CHURCH. DAY

STELLA *comes into the church. She wears a dark suit. People are seated. Heads turn as her heels clip up the aisle. She carries a bouquet of tulips and white lilac.* HARRISON *is sitting alone at the back of the church. She sits and looks at the coffin. An organ plays.*

EXT. GRAVEYARD. DAY

In long shot a group is turning from a grave and walking towards the road. STELLA *walks alone. She looks back and glimpses* HARRISON *'stepping cranelike' over the graves.*
A man catches up with STELLA.

BLYTHE
Mrs Rodney?

STELLA
Yes?

BLYTHE
My name is Blythe. I am – I was – Mr Morris's lawyer.

STELLA
Ah.

BLYTHE
Your son wasn't able to come?

STELLA
He's in the army.

BLYTHE
Yes, quite. When we get to the hotel – I should be obliged if you would give me a few minutes of your time for a private word?

STELLA

Yes . . .

BLYTHE

Have you any idea who that man is, by the way?

STELLA

No.

BLYTHE

Nobody knows him.

EXT. VILLAGE: MAIN STREET. DAY

The group walking along the pavement past empty shop windows. MRS TRINGSBY *shepherds two elderly ladies, precisely dressed, who walk arm in arm.*
A fishmonger's slab empty; a baker's shop empty; a greengrocer's shop with fans of cardboard bananas and a DIG FOR VICTORY *placard; a butcher's shop with a few joints of purplish meat; sign on window of empty newspaper shop:* NO MATCHES.
The group enters the hotel.

INT. HOTEL: LADIES' CLOAKROOM. DAY

MRS TRINGSBY *and* STELLA *taking off coats.*

MRS TRINGSBY

Are you a relation of Mr Morris?

STELLA

He was my husband's cousin.

MRS TRINGSBY

He dropped dead in my house. Can you believe it? We'd hardly been introduced. I mean, he had only been in the house five minutes. Can you imagine?
She indicates the LADIES.

These are two of my oldest house-guests. I've brought them out for a little treat. Are you having a nice little treat?
The LADIES *smile.*

INT. HOTEL: LANDING. DAY

They emerge from the cloakroom. BLYTHE *approaches.*

BLYTHE
Mrs Rodney, might I have that word?
He takes STELLA *into a recess.*
I thought you should know straightaway that in his will Mr Morris left all his estate to your son Roderick. There is an existing trust for his widow, of course. But apart from that, his house, land and capital go to your son.

STELLA
Good gracious.

BLYTHE
This is a copy of the will. As he is still under twenty-one, you are of course his guardian.
STELLA *takes the envelope, looks at it, looks at* BLYTHE.

STELLA
But I can't . . . They never met . . . Why do you think . . . ?

BLYTHE
He knew no other young person. I believe he wanted to leave his estate to a young person – in the hope that he may care in his own way to carry on the old tradition. And they were, of course, cousins.

STELLA
Yes. Yes, they were.

CALDERDALE
COLLEGE LIBRARY
HALIFAX

INT. HOTEL: LUNCHROOM. DAY

A table with a simple buffet. BLYTHE *and* STELLA *come into the room. People turn, look curiously at* STELLA. *Some whisper.*
HARRISON *stands alone at the window.*
BLYTHE *gives* STELLA *a cup of coffee. Someone calls his name. He turns.*

BLYTHE

(*To* STELLA)
Excuse me.
She sips her coffee. Suddenly HARRISON *is at her side.*

HARRISON

Can I get you some port?
She turns to him.
They do have port here – or at least they call it port.

STELLA

No thank you, I –

HARRISON

Or there's a bar downstairs.

STELLA

Don't let me stop you.

HARRISON

My name's Harrison. You're Mrs Rodney – am I right?

STELLA

Yes. I'm sorry . . . but how do you know my name is Rodney?

HARRISON

Well, there's no one else here who could be you, is there? I've heard your praises sung a good deal, you see.

STELLA

Who by?

HARRISON

Your cousin, Frankie.

STELLA

Oh, you knew him?

HARRISON

Oh yes. Very well. I used to go to see him in Ireland. Great old house. Do you remember it?

STELLA

I haven't been there for . . . many years.

HARRISON

On your honeymoon, wasn't it? It's to go to your son – I seem to remember?

STELLA

Yes, I –

HARRISON

Yes, he told me all about you, old Frankie. Told me you were a widow – had a boy – everything. He was really very fond of you. Used to talk about you a lot.

STELLA

Did he? But . . . if I'd known that . . . If I'd known he remembered me I could have gone to see him . . . taken my son. I didn't know, you see.

HARRISON

Yes. Pity. One so often thinks of things too late.

STELLA

Excuse me.
She turns away, calls:

Mr Blythe? Mr Blythe, can I have a word?

EXT. COUNTRY ROAD. DAY

STELLA *walking alone towards the station.*

EXT. COUNTRY STATION: PLATFORM. DAY

STELLA *standing alone at the end of the platform. A voice: 'First smoker?' She turns sharply. It is* HARRISON.

STELLA
I'm travelling third.

HARRISON
Oh, come on! Let's blow the expense – in honour of Frankie. It's on the house anyway.
The train comes in.

INT. TRAIN: FIRST-CLASS COMPARTMENT. DAY

STELLA *and* HARRISON *come in and sit facing each other.*

HARRISON
It's not every day, you know, that one runs into someone one's been wanting to meet for so long. It's quite an event.

STELLA
What do you do?

HARRISON
What do I do?

STELLA
Yes.

HARRISON

Government work.

EXT. COUNTRY STATION: PLATFORM. DAY

The stationary train. Two RAF OFFICERS *run up the platform and jump on.*

INT. TRAIN: FIRST-CLASS COMPARTMENT. DAY

HARRISON *smiles, leans forward.*

HARRISON

Yes, I'd like to meet your son.

STELLA

Really? Why?

HARRISON

Well, somehow he seems . . . all that's left of old Frankie.

STELLA

Oh.

HARRISON

I'd like to get to know you both as a matter of fact – as a family.

STELLA

I'm sorry, I don't understand –
The door opens. The two RAF OFFICERS *enter, sit, lean back, close their eyes.*
STELLA *speaks in a lower voice.*
I don't understand your . . . interest . . . in us.

HARRISON

Well, I could explain it – I could explain one aspect of it – if you like. I'll tell you what – when we get to town –

CALDERDALE
COLLEGE LIBRARY
HALIFAX

why don't I take you home in a taxi and we could have a chat?

STELLA

(*Non-committal*) Mmmn–hmmn.

She looks out of the window. The platform is empty. The train does not move. She closes her eyes.

HARRISON *watches her, lights a cigarette.*

INT. KING'S CROSS STATION: PLATFORM. DAY

HARRISON *and* STELLA *walking along the platform.*

HARRISON

Listen. I'll dash ahead to the rank and grab a taxi. All right? See you there.

He runs on. She turns right out of the platform and goes down the stairs to the Underground.

INT. ROOM

Hand sifting photographs:

Long shot of STELLA *at the entrance to the King's Cross Underground.*

ROBERT *going up steps to* STELLA*'s front door.*

ROBERT *and two men at the bar of a pub.*

ROBERT *and* STELLA *at a restaurant table.*

Hand puts this photograph aside.

STELLA *in the graveyard.*

STELLA *on the Underground platform.*

The hand pins the last two photographs to the wall.
Over this, button A in telephone box is pressed.
HARRISON*'s voice.*

HARRISON

Hello, Mrs Rodney?

STELLA

Yes?

HARRISON

It's Harrison.

STELLA

I can't hear you. Speak up.

HARRISON

It's Harrison. I hope you got home safely – the other day.

STELLA

Yes. Thank you.

HARRISON

Listen, I would like to come and see you actually – have a word – there is something – really quite important to talk about – how about – ?

STELLA

What do you mean? What do you mean, important?

HARRISON

Well . . . it's just quite important.
Silence on the line.
Eight o'clock on Sunday?
Silence on the line.

EXT. REGENT'S PARK OPEN-AIR THEATRE. EARLY EVENING

A Viennese orchestra playing.
HARRISON *sitting, thrusting his right fist into his left palm spasmodically.* LOUIE *next to him, wearing an imitation camel-hair coat. A* CZECH SOLDIER. *Vacant seats between them.*
The orchestra stops playing. Mild applause. LOUIE *looks at a programme sheet. She turns to* HARRISON.

LOUIE

Was that number seven they've just played or number eight?

He does not reply.

Can you tell from the programme? Would you like to see my programme?

HARRISON

No thanks.

LOUIE

Sorry I spoke.

He turns and looks at her.

HARRISON

Have we met?

LOUIE

How do you mean, 'met'?

HARRISON

We don't know each other?

LOUIE

I've never seen you before in my life.

HARRISON

Then that settles that, doesn't it?

LOUIE

Why? Are you someone special? I'll know you from now on anyway. I never forget a face. Do you?

HARRISON

I could easily.

The band starts to play.

INT. STELLA'S FLAT. EVENING

STELLA *at the window playing with the blind cord. She looks down into Weymouth Street. Eight o'clock strikes. She walks to the mantelpiece, looks in the mirror at herself, glances at photographs on the shelf of* ROBERT *and* RODERICK, *both in uniform.*

EXT. THE PARK. EVENING

Eight o'clock striking.
HARRISON *stands and walks away.* LOUIE *stands, joins him.*

LOUIE

I've had enough too.
She looks at the lawns.
Look at all the shadows. It really looks ghostly, doesn't it?

HARRISON

Goodnight then.

LOUIE

Yes, I'm going home.

HARRISON

Good idea.
They walk on together.

LOUIE

Are you?

HARRISON

Am I what?

LOUIE

Going home.
HARRISON *stops.*

HARRISON

Listen. You'll end up in trouble one of these days. Tacking on like this. There are funny people about. Don't you know that?

LOUIE

I told you, I'm going home.

HARRISON

Well, which way do you live?

LOUIE

Oh, I can go any way really.
They walk into the outer circle.

HARRISON

All right. I go this way. (*He points.*) You go that way.

LOUIE

Yes, that's right.
He turns.
Wait a minute.

HARRISON

What?

LOUIE

I don't know your name.

HARRISON

No. You don't.
He turns and walks away. She stands.

INT. THE FLAT. EVENING

STELLA *waiting. She hears a door bang below. Footsteps. Finally* HARRISON *appears at the open door of her flat. He looks in, sees her.*

HARRISON

Good evening.

STELLA

Good evening.

HARRISON

I found the downstairs door on the latch. That in order?

STELLA

I left it open for you.

HARRISON

I shut it. That in order too?

STELLA

Why don't you shut this one?
He comes into the room and shuts the door.
How did you get my telephone number?

HARRISON

Oh . . . I think I met a man who knew you. Look, are you sure this is a convenient time?

STELLA

It's not in the least convenient. No time would be convenient. You said you had something important to say to me. What is it?
He looks round the room, murmurs.

HARRISON

All your things are so pretty.
He suddenly switches on a lamp. She goes to the windows quickly, lowers the blackout blinds. She turns. He is looking at the photographs on the mantelpiece.
This your son?

STELLA

Yes.
He picks up the photograph of ROBERT.

HARRISON

Mmmnn. Yes, this is quite a good likeness.

STELLA

What do you mean?
Pause
Do you know him?

HARRISON

I know *of* him. Know him by sight. We haven't actually met.

STELLA

By sight?

HARRISON

Yes. I've seen him around . . . you know . . . around . . . sometimes with you, in fact. I'd seen him with you a number of times – before you and I met.

STELLA

Oh really?

HARRISON

That's right, yes.

STELLA

Will you please tell me what you've come to say?
He lights a cigarette.

HARRISON

You should be a bit more careful who you know.

STELLA

In general?

HARRISON

In particular.

STELLA

I am. I didn't want to know you, for example.

HARRISON

Have a cigarette.

She takes one. He lights a match. His hand is shaking. She looks at his hand.

Yes . . . funny . . . that doesn't happen very often. Must be being here with you, all on our own.

STELLA

What do you want?

HARRISON

Well, I'll tell you. I want you to give me a break. That's all. I want you to let me come here, be here, be in and out of here, on and off, all the time. I want to be in your life, as they say. In your life. Except . . .

He puts the photograph of ROBERT *face down on the shelf.*

. . . less of that. In fact none of that at all. No more of that.

She stares at him and laughs.

STELLA

You're a lunatic.

HARRISON

No, no. That's simply what I want, you see. That's what I want you to think about. Seriously.

STELLA

You want me to think about it seriously.

CALDERDALE
COLLEGE LIBRARY
HALIFAX

HARRISON

Well, yes I do. Because if you don't – your friend could be in a lot of trouble. As against that, if you and I could arrange things between us, things . . . might be arranged.

STELLA

Oh, for Christ's sake get to the point! What the hell are you talking about.
Silence.

HARRISON

Your friend's been playing the fool. He *is* playing the fool, I should say. Look. As you know, he's at the War Office. That's probably all you do know. But I know a little more than that. I'll tell you what he does. He gives information to the enemy. The gist of the stuff he handles is getting through to the enemy. This has been . . . satisfactorily verified. He's working for the enemy.

STELLA

This is silly.

HARRISON

I've been watching him, you see. I . . . keep my eye on him. And – the way things are – I could tip the scales either way. The thing could just turn on the stuff I send up. Or don't send up. You follow? I'm holding quite a bit of stuff on him I haven't turned in yet. It doesn't *have* to go in. They don't know it exists. Perhaps you could help me decide.
Pause.
What I'm saying is this – what finally happens to him rather depends on me. Or when I say it rather depends on me I mean it rather depends on you. Do you see?

STELLA

Yes. I see.

HARRISON

Oh, you do? Good.

STELLA

Perfectly. I'm to sleep with you in order that a man be left free to go on selling his country.

HARRISON

That's putting it a bit crudely.

STELLA

Anyway, none of this matters because we're not talking about the same man. You *are* crazy. When did you think this up?

HARRISON

You don't believe me?
She laughs shortly.

STELLA

No.

HARRISON

Why not?

STELLA

If this story were true – if you are what you say you are – would you tell *me*, of all people, knowing I'd go straight to Robert with the whole thing? What else would you expect?

HARRISON

Well, I'd expect someone like you to be more intelligent. If you warn him and we know you warn him, he's no more use to us and we pull him in. You see? That's the end of him. So I wouldn't warn him if I were you.

STELLA

What do you mean – 'we know you warn him'? How would you know? I wouldn't tell you.

HARRISON

It would stick out a mile. If you warn him, he'll change his timetable. He'll alter his course, he'll throw a smoke screen. We'd know he'd been tipped the wink and we'd pull him in.

STELLA

But if I warned him of that? What if I told him *not* to change his . . . course in any way?

HARRISON

That would take a lot of nerve and some tiptop acting. How much of an actor is he? That's the question.

STELLA

Actor? What do you mean? He's never acted with me.

HARRISON

Ah. No. No, I suppose not.

STELLA

No.

HARRISON

Well . . . yes . . . if a man were able to act being in love, he'd be enough of an actor to get away with anything. Wouldn't he?

Pause.

Anyway, coming back to where we were . . . My only point is . . . if you warned him you'd sink him.

STELLA

Give me another cigarette.

He does so and lights it. His hand is still shaking.

Your hand is still shaking.

She smokes.
So you're a counter-spy, are you? A key man. And you're on the track of a man working for the enemy. And your employers trust you. Don't they? What would your employers say, I wonder, if they knew what you were up to? If they knew that by becoming your mistress I can buy out a man who you say is a traitor to his country? What view would they take of that? Why shouldn't I report you? You would be sorry, you say, if I sank Robert. How would it be if I sank you?

HARRISON

You could. Absolutely. You could sink me. But it all comes back to the same old thing. If you sink me you sink him.
STELLA *turns and picks* ROBERT'S *photograph up so that it faces the room.*

STELLA

(*Savagely*) How dare you touch this photograph! How dare you!
They stare at each other.
The telephone rings. She picks it up.
Hello? . . . Roderick! . . . Where are you? . . . Wonderful . . . Yes, of course . . . Have you eaten? There's nothing . . . Oh, right . . . Yes, as soon as you can.
She puts the phone down.
That was my son. He's on leave. He's on his way round here.

HARRISON

That's nice for you. Look, there's no hurry about all of this. Take a bit of time to think it over.

STELLA

You seriously expect me . . . ?

HARRISON

Oh, you might as well think it over. And – if it suited you – I might drop in from time to time. Who knows? I might grow on you.

HARRISON *goes to the door and leaves the flat.*

EXT. WEYMOUTH STREET. NIGHT

RODERICK *walks down the street with kitbag. He turns the corner. A figure under a lamp-post lights a cigarette.* HARRISON.

INT. THE FLAT. NIGHT

RODERICK *dumping kit inside the door. He kisses* STELLA.

RODERICK

Can I have a bath?

STELLA

Yes, go on, while I make coffee.

RODERICK

Any cake?

STELLA

Biscuits. Are you starving?

RODERICK

No, no. Fred knew of a pub that had pork pies.

INT. THE FLAT. NIGHT

RODERICK *comes out of the bathroom wearing a dressing-gown.*

RODERICK

Robert won't mind if I wear his dressing-gown, will he?

STELLA *comes out of the kitchen with coffee.*

STELLA

Of course not.

RODERICK

(*Muttering*) I think I've got a corn.

STELLA

I wish there was something for you to eat. There are only three biscuits.

RODERICK *sits on the sofa.*

Roderick – is that a corn?

RODERICK

I think so.

STELLA

Does it hurt?

RODERICK

Absolutely excruciating.

She half rises.

STELLA

I've got a plaster –

He stops her.

RODERICK

No, really. I want to ask you something. In Ireland – at the house – my house – there's a river –

STELLA

Yes.

CALDERDALE
COLLEGE LIBRARY
HALIFAX

RODERICK

Is there a boat?

STELLA

A boat?

RODERICK

Don't you know?

STELLA

I haven't been there for twenty years! But I remember the river.

RODERICK

I can picture it. I can see it – in my mind's eye. When we go, I'll row you down the river. Shall I?

STELLA

If there's a boat.

RODERICK

Oh, there must be.

RODERICK *suddenly glances at the cigarette ends in an ashtray.*

Someone been here?

STELLA

What?

RODERICK

Someone's been here.

STELLA

Yes. A man called Harrison.

RODERICK

Who's he?

STELLA

No one. A bore.

He suddenly sneezes.

Oh dear.

He sneezes again.

RODERICK

Handkerchief.

He puts his hand into the pocket of the gown, brings out a piece of folded notepaper. He looks at it.

STELLA

Here's a handkerchief.

RODERICK

Thanks.

STELLA

Put it back.

RODERICK

What?

STELLA

Put that piece of paper back. Into the pocket. It's not yours. Just . . . put it back.

RODERICK

Oh. Well, why don't you take it? It might fall out again.

STELLA

It didn't *fall* out this time.

RODERICK

But it might next time and . . . you know . . .

STELLA

You know what?

RODERICK

Well, it might be important. Top Secret or something. Isn't what Robert's doing important?
She takes the paper from him, makes to tear it up.
Hey! It isn't yours either.
She stops.
Shall we have a peep? See what it says? Just for fun.

STELLA

No.

RODERICK

Why not?

STELLA

(*Smiling*) It might be a letter from another woman.

RODERICK

Oh, I wouldn't think so.
Silence.
Look, don't you think it would be best if I just put it back into the pocket? After all, as you said, it's Robert's . . . thing . . . and it's his pocket.
STELLA *unfolds the paper and reads.*

STELLA

Nothing.
She tears it across.

INT. TRAIN COMPARTMENT. DAY

STELLA *looking out of the window. She turns quickly, smiles.*
ROBERT *sitting opposite her. He smiles.*

STELLA

What did you tell them?

ROBERT

I told them you were someone working in a government office and that you liked country hikes.

STELLA

Country hikes! But look at these shoes.

ROBERT

I like them.

STELLA

Well, they're hardly shoes for a hike.
ROBERT *laughs.*

ROBERT

They're fine. Really. Anyway, it hardly matters.

STELLA

You mean we don't *have* to go for a hike.

ROBERT

No, no. We're free. Quite free. (*He takes her hand.*) They're harmless. Honestly. Anyway, I'll protect you if mother tries to bite you.

STELLA

Will you?

EXT. COUNTRY ROAD. DAY

A taxi stops. ROBERT *and* STELLA *get out.* ROBERT *pays. The taxi drives away.*
Notice: CAUTION: CONCEALED DRIVE.
They walk up the drive towards Holme Dene. Evergreens. Lawns leading to the house. ROBERT *walks with a limp.* ERNESTINE *suddenly appears around a bush, laughing heartily.*

ROBERT

Hello, Ernie!

ERNESTINE *laughs. She is in WVS uniform.*

ERNESTINE

What did you do with the taxi?

ROBERT

We walked from the road.

ERNESTINE

Oh, of course – you've come down to walk, haven't you?

ROBERT

Ernestine – Mrs Rodney.

They shake hands. ERNESTINE *roars with laughter.*

ERNESTINE

Muttikins is in the lounge – waiting for the sound of the taxi! (*To* STELLA) We were only saying this morning that it took being shot in the leg to make Robert walk! See you both at tea.

She goes down the drive. They walk towards the house.

STELLA

What was she laughing at?

ROBERT

Oh . . . just laughing. Muttikins is my mother. That's what we call her.

INT. THE HOUSE: LOUNGE. DAY

MRS KELWAY *with knitting.* ROBERT *and* STELLA *come in. She stands.* ROBERT *bends to her. They kiss.*

MRS KELWAY

Robert . . .

ROBERT

Muttikins . . . This is Mrs Rodney.

MRS KELWAY *frowns.*

MRS KELWAY

Mrs Rodney?

She looks at STELLA. STELLA *puts out her hand.*

STELLA

How do you do?

They shake hands. MRS KELWAY *turns to* ROBERT.

MRS KELWAY

But what became of the taxi?

ROBERT

We walked up the drive.

MRS KELWAY

Ernestine was listening for it. Did she miss you?

ROBERT

No, we ran into her – a little *détraquée.*

MRS KELWAY

It is Saturday afternoon.

MRS KELWAY *sits.* ROBERT *sits. After a moment* STELLA *sits.*

If I hadn't seen you walking up the drive I should have wondered if you hadn't missed the train.

ROBERT

Mrs Rodney likes to walk in the country.

STELLA

It's so nice to be out of London.

MRS KELWAY

I've hardly been up to London since the war began. I've always understood that we're asked not to travel without a good reason. I'm quite content to sit here and knit.
She knits.
My grandson is in the army. Ernestine's boy.

STELLA

So is my son.
MRS KELWAY *continues to knit.*

ROBERT

Roderick.
MRS KELWAY *looks up at him.*

MRS KELWAY

What do you mean by 'Roderick'?

ROBERT

Roderick is Mrs Rodney's son.

MRS KELWAY

Oh.
Silence.

ROBERT

(*To* STELLA) A breath of air?

MRS KELWAY

Tea will be coming in.

ROBERT

A stroll before tea.

EXT. THE GARDEN. DAY

ROBERT *and* STELLA *stroll across the lawn. She looks at him. He looks at her. She smiles. He laughs.*

INT. THE HOUSE: LOUNGE. DAY

MRS KELWAY, ROBERT, STELLA, PETER *(aged nine)* and ANNE *(aged seven) sitting at a mahogany table.* MRS KELWAY *is pouring and passing tea. Silence.*
STELLA *turns and looks out of the window to see* ERNESTINE *running towards the house. She rushes into the room.*

ERNESTINE

Oh dear, I'm late! Is the bread cut yet? No! Just in time!
She sits, saws at the loaf and passes slices round the table on the flat of the knife.

ROBERT

Mrs Rodney and I forgot to bring our own butter.

STELLA

I don't often eat tea . . . actually.

ERNESTINE

Well, I suppose I could lend you some of my butter. But really I don't think it would stand up in court.
ROBERT *splits open a bun and spreads damson jam on it.*

PETER

Look at all that jam!

ANNE

Do you always do that? I mean, do you always use so much jam in London?

ROBERT

Sure. (*He winks.*) I get it on the black market.

ANNE

You might end up in prison.

CALDERDALE
COLLEGE LIBRARY
HALIFAX

ROBERT

Well, you'll have to come and visit me in my cell, won't you?

ANNE

I don't want to!

ERNESTINE

We shall be having tears in a minute.

MRS KELWAY

If it's not too much trouble, Granny would like some bread.

ERNESTINE

Oh Muttikins! Didn't I give you any?

STELLA

(*To* PETER) What do those letters on your armlet stand for?

PETER

It's top secret.

ERNESTINE

Did I see you wearing your armlet *outside* the gate?

PETER

We kept under cover.

ERNESTINE

Under cover or not, this is a serious war. You have to obey orders. Now, ask Mrs Rodney if she would like some more tea. If she says 'yes' pass her cup and don't drop the spoon.

PETER

Would you – ?

MRS KELWAY

Mrs Rodney doesn't care for afternoon tea.

STELLA *looks at her.*

STELLA

Oh, I . . . do drink quite a lot of tea in the office.

MRS KELWAY

We now drink tea only once a day. Otherwise we might not have enough for guests. (*She sips.*) If it weren't for the children I should be tempted to do without tea altogether – I mean drum it out of the house. Mind you, it can become extraordinarily cold here. (*To Stella*) The fuel shortage. And so one does benefit from a hot beverage. (*She looks at* ERNESTINE.) My daughter doesn't feel the cold. She moves about so much she seldom takes her hat off. Robert tells me that in London you wouldn't notice the war. That's far from the case here, I can assure you. But I'm glad Robert is enjoying a period of calm. He went through so much. So much. More than we care to speak of.

ERNESTINE

Mum's the word here. Isn't that so, children?

ROBERT *slices a piece of cake and offers it to* STELLA.

ROBERT

Cake?

STELLA

No thanks.

ANNE

Why not? Do you think it will make you fat?

ERNESTINE

Mrs Rodney is free not to eat cake if she doesn't want to. That's the difference between England and Germany.

PETER

The Nazis would force her to eat cake.

ERNESTINE *laughs loudly.*

ROBERT

(*To* STELLA) Come and see the house.

ERNESTINE *laughs even more loudly.*

ERNESTINE

Isn't it time for your walk?

ROBERT

House first.

ERNESTINE

But there's nothing to see in the house! Honestly! What a waste of a fine afternoon.

ROBERT

Mrs Rodney is interested in interior decoration.

MRS KELWAY

(*To* STELLA) I'm afraid we have nothing of that sort here.

ROBERT

Then I shall show her my photographs.

ERNESTINE

Won't Mrs Rodney think you're very vain?

PETER

Can we come too?

ROBERT

No. Go outside and I'll see you from the window.

ERNESTINE

The house is up for sale anyway. It's too big.

ROBERT *and* STELLA *walk to the door.*

MRS KELWAY

You should warn Mrs Rodney that the better rooms are all shut up. Because of the war.

INT. THE HOUSE: STAIRCASE. DAY

ROBERT *and* STELLA *ascending.*

ROBERT

Don't think you're making a bad impression. I assure you you're making no impression at all.
They proceed up the attic stairs to his room.

INT. ROBERT'S ROOM. DAY

ROBERT *and* STELLA *come into the room.*
A 'varsity' chair padded. A swivel lamp. Glass cases of coins, birds' eggs, fossils, butterflies. Trophies in a pyramid over the chimney-piece. On two walls in passe-partout *or in frames sixty or seventy photographs, all featuring* ROBERT *at various ages.*
STELLA *looks at the photographs and laughs.*

STELLA

Good gracious! Did you – hang all these up?

ROBERT

No. But, as you see, I haven't taken them down. My mother and Ernie put them there.

STELLA

They really must be very fond of you.

ROBERT

No, it's not that. They expect me to be very fond of myself.

STELLA

But . . . are you? I don't think you are.

She examines the photographs.

Is this Susannah?

ROBERT

Yes.

STELLA

I don't see anything wrong with her.

ROBERT *is silent.*

And this? Is this your father?

ROBERT

Yes.

She looks about the room.

STELLA

Very odd. The room feels . . . empty.

ROBERT

Yes. It is. Each time I come into it I'm hit in the face by the feeling that I don't exist. That I never have existed. So it's extraordinary coming in here with you. Gives me a kind of vertigo. I can't explain it.

She points to the photographs.

STELLA

But there – there is your existence.

ROBERT

That's not my existence. That's my criminal record. A senseless criminal record. Don't you think? I know it by heart. A naked baby. Smirking over that tournament cup. In shorts on top of a rock with Thompson. An usher at Amabelle's wedding. Picnicking with Susannah. Larking about with Ernie's Labrador. Playing cricket with Dad. God! Can you think of a better way of driving a man mad than nailing that pack of his own lies all round the room where he has to sleep?

STELLA

Then why don't you take them down?

ROBERT

They would hate that.

She opens a drawer in a chest of drawers and lifts folded tissue paper.

STELLA

Ah. Socks. Beautifully preserved.

She sits on the window seat.

What was your father like?

ROBERT

He was like Ernie's Labrador. Ernie's Labrador died halfway through Munich week. He was very sensitive. So was my father. In all but one sense he was impotent. He let himself be buckled into his marriage like Ernie's Labrador let himself be buckled into his collar. My father's death was a great relief. To me, that is. And probably to him.

Sound of children from below. STELLA *looks out of the window.*

EXT. THE GARDEN. DAY

The children march into view performing military exercises. ROBERT *calls down.*

ROBERT

Don't hold your breath for too long!

ANNE *opens her mouth, exhales and collapses on the lawn.*

PETER *calls up to the window.*

PETER

Nobody can find the half-ounce weight off the weighing machine!

ANNE

Granny wanted to weigh the parcel for you to post in London!

PETER

You'll have to have it weighed *in* London!

ANNE

She can't weigh it because she can't find the weight!

INT. ROBERT'S ROOM. DAY

ERNESTINE *bursts into the room.*

ERNESTINE

Yes, here you are!

ROBERT

Yes, indeed. Why?

ERNESTINE

I thought you had gone on your walk, until I heard the children shouting. Thank goodness I caught you. Muttikins has a parcel for you to post in London. For Christopher.

ROBERT

What's the matter with the post office here?

ERNESTINE

Nothing. But it's closed on Sunday and in London they're open.

ROBERT

Are they?

ERNESTINE

Well, some are.

STELLA

I'd love to post the parcel.
They look at her.

ROBERT

But it can wait until we're actually . . . leaving, can't it?

ERNESTINE

Ah well, you see, (a) there's almost always a rush at the last moment and (b) I may have to dash off myself soon. But the point is – there's been a complication. Nobody can find the little half-ounce weight off the weighing machine. Literally nobody. Muttikins is far from sure that she may not have understamped the parcel. So the plan is this – she will leave three pennies with the parcel, just in case, on the oak chest in front of the stairs. If you find the parcel is *not*, repeat *not* understamped you can give her back the pennies the next time you're here. Is that clear? Shall I get the children to remind you?

ROBERT

No. It's clear.

ERNESTINE

(*To* STELLA) How do you like our gallery?

STELLA

It's quite a . . .

ERNESTINE

Robert has always photographed well. Crooked again! (*She dashes to straighten some photos.*) Did Robert tell you that this is our sister Amabelle, the children's mother,

CALDERDALE
COLLEGE LIBRARY
HALIFAX

caught in India for the duration? And this is our father – oh he used to radiate such energy and fun – in some ways Robert takes after him. And that, poor fellow, was my dog.

STELLA

Yes, so Robert said.

ERNESTINE

He had such faith in human nature. I often think that if Hitler could have looked into that dog's eyes, the story might have been very different. Hark! There goes the telephone! Someone's after me!
She dashes out.
ROBERT *and* STELLA *look at each other.*

EXT. LONDON STREET. NIGHT

STELLA *walking through deserted streets with parcel. Occasional figures in doorways. Lovers 'blotted' together.*
She crosses Langham Place into Weymouth Street. She walks towards her house, falters, stops, peers into the dark.
A match is struck, sheltered, thrown away.
She walks on, goes up the steps.

STELLA

Been waiting long?

HARRISON

I thought you'd be back about now.
She opens the front door. He slips up the steps.
I'd rather like a word, if I may?
She looks at him, goes in. He follows.

INT. HALL. NIGHT

The door closes. Darkness.
She climbs the stairs. A torch follows her, lights her path. When they reach the door to her flat, the beam plays on her fingers as she unlocks the door.
They go in.

INT. THE FLAT. NIGHT

She draws the blackout blinds, pulls the curtains, switches on lamps and the electric fire. She turns.
HARRISON *is sitting.*

HARRISON
Nice to be here again. You know, I really feel at home.

STELLA
In that case, I shall change my shoes.
She goes into the bedroom.
He sits, lights a cigarette.
She returns, wearing mules.
I've been in the country, as I expect you know.

HARRISON
Making the most of the last of the fine weather?

STELLA
What do you mean by that?

HARRISON
Were you making the most of the last of the fine weather?
She leans back, puts her feet up on a stool, sighs.
You seem more relaxed tonight.

STELLA
I'm extremely tired.

HARRISON

Must have been quite a day. How did it go?

STELLA

How did what go?

HARRISON

Look, you don't have to talk, if you don't want to. I'll be quite happy just sitting here.

STELLA

Why? Is this your evening off?

HARRISON

I don't quite –

STELLA

Is this business or pleasure?

HARRISON *leans forward, begins to push his fist into the palm of his hand.*

Why don't you tell me what else I've been doing?

HARRISON

Well, one thing I know you've been doing, Stella – you've been thinking things over.

STELLA

Have I?

HARRISON

Yes. You've thought things over. Today you did exactly what I should have done. You went to look at the first place where rot could start. The home hearth. I wonder what you found? I wouldn't dream of asking you, of course.

Pause.

STELLA

I haven't . . . said anything . . . to him about . . .

HARRISON

Oh, I know that. He hasn't changed his habits, you see. He's doing the same things. The only change is you. You're not as natural on the telephone at nights as you used to be. Anyone would think you thought his line was being tapped.
She looks at him.

STELLA

So that's what you do in the evenings.
Pause.

HARRISON

And how have you got on with your other check-up – on me?

STELLA

I haven't got very far.

HARRISON

The thing is, not all that many people know who I am.
He suddenly looks at the parcel.
What's this?

STELLA

It's a parcel – for posting. I should have taken it to a post office. I was too tired.

HARRISON

Would you like me to post it for you?

STELLA

Would you? Oh . . . thank you. That would be one thing . . . less . . .

HARRISON

Leave it to me.

She lies back. He gazes at her.

The first time I saw you . . . you were lying quite like this . . . on the grass in Regent's Park. Your eyes were closed. Then you opened your eyes and you looked up at the sky. You didn't know I was watching every move you made.

STELLA

And was that when you . . . ?

HARRISON

Yes. That's when. And then it got worse. And then I met you at the funeral and it was even worse. And now it's hell.

STELLA

Hell?

HARRISON

Yes. It's hell!

He punches his fist.

We're getting nowhere!

STELLA

You mean I'm wasting your time? What a joke. You come round and waste my time by telling me I'm wasting yours. What the hell do you expect from me? Sympathy?

Pause.

HARRISON

You know, I feel that we're getting to know each other. We're not so unlike – underneath.

STELLA

You're right. We're horribly alike. You've succeeded in making a spy of me.

He stands abruptly, goes to the window, opens the

curtains and goes through them. The curtains swing into place behind him.
She hears the blind go up. A breath of wind. Silence.
She stands, goes to the curtains, through the curtains, holds the curtain aside, looks for him. Light flashes on the pane.

HARRISON

Mind. Either come through or go back.
She drops the curtain. They stand together in the alcove in the dark.

STELLA

What are you doing?

HARRISON

It's raining.
He puts his hand out of the window.
It's not going to stop.

STELLA

Have you . . . far to go?

HARRISON

It depends where I go.

STELLA

Where do you live?

HARRISON

Oh . . . there are always two or three places where I can turn in.

STELLA

Where do you keep your razor?

HARRISON

I've got more than one razor.
Silence.

Ah, that air's good. I needed a breath of air.

STELLA

Breathe it . . . for as long as you like.

HARRISON

Stay with me. You breathe too.
They stand.
I can feel you breathing.
They are still.
Abruptly, she goes back through the curtains. He follows.

STELLA

I'm tired.

HARRISON

Leave your parcel to me. I'll deal with it.

STELLA

Listen. If I wanted to find you – how would I find you?

HARRISON

Don't worry about finding me. I'll be in touch.
He goes.

EXT. REGENT'S PARK. DAY

ROBERT *and* STELLA *walking fast.*

ROBERT

I'm sorry, I just don't see why you have to go at all.

STELLA

It's for a few days. That's all.

ROBERT

I don't want you to go away at all! Ever! Anywhere!
Without me. Don't you understand?

STELLA

You don't think I want to go? I don't. In fact I dread it. But it's simply business for Roderick. It's not a matter of feeling.

ROBERT

Isn't dread a feeling?

STELLA

Someone's got to go. He can't – I must. Someone's got to look at the place, the roof . . . all that. Oh really, Robert, I've been through more than enough convincing the Passport Office – do I have to go through it all over again with you?

ROBERT

The Passport Office is not in love with you.

STELLA

Weeks ago, you agreed I would have to go.

ROBERT

Did I? Yes, I suppose I did.

STELLA

Has anything changed since then?
They stop by a tree.

ROBERT

Changed? No. Nothing's changed.
He takes her face in his hands and kisses her.
But what will you do while you're away? Will you keep loving me?

STELLA

I'll keep loving you.

CALDERDALE
COLLEGE LIBRARY
HALIFAX

INT. HARRISON'S ROOM

Photographs of STELLA *on the wall. One lamp. Cigarette smoke. The camera focuses on a photograph of* ROBERT *kissing* STELLA *in the park.*

EXT. COUNTRY ROAD. DAY

RODERICK *walking towards Wistaria Lodge.*

EXT. WISTARIA LODGE. DAY

RODERICK *at the door. It opens.* MRS TRINGSBY.

RODERICK

Good afternoon.

MRS TRINGSBY

I am Mrs Tringsby. You are not . . . Mr Rodney, are you?

RODERICK

Yes, I am.

MRS TRINGSBY

Oh dear. I had expected you to be rather older and not quite so early. However, do by all means come into the drawing room.

INT. THE HALL. DAY

The door closes.

RODERICK

Is my cousin in there?

MRS TRINGSBY

No, oh dear no. She likes to be cosy in her room. She knows she is going to have a treat of some kind today but you may find she has forgotten what.

RODERICK

Then I can go up?

MRS TRINGSBY

I *should* like one word with you first, if you don't mind.
They go into the drawing room.

INT. DRAWING ROOM. DAY

MRS TRINGSBY

We are not making difficulties – but please remember what happened last time.

RODERICK

Last time?

MRS TRINGSBY

Last time she had a visitor. It was such a dreadful shock to us all.

RODERICK

Yes, I know. I'm sorry. In fact I'm sure Cousin Francis would want me to apologize.

MRS TRINGSBY

He should never have come!

RODERICK

Does Cousin Nettie know he's dead?

MRS TRINGSBY

This dear room will never quite feel the same to me again.

RODERICK

Oh, that sort of thing doesn't happen twice. And the Army could tell you I'm as sound as a bell.

MRS TRINGSBY

Yes, that's another thing – I mean, your coming down here in uniform. We're so careful here not to have dreadful thoughts. You won't on any account talk to Mrs Morris about the war, will you? Just a light chat. And never, of course, mention the past.

RODERICK

I want to talk about the future. Is this the way?

INT. STAIRS. DAY

They go up to the first landing. She whispers.

MRS TRINGSBY

She may not know who you are.

RODERICK

I relied on you to tell her.

MRS TRINGSBY

Oh, I told her – but . . .
She knocks on a door.
Here we are!
She opens the door and goes in.
Hello! Here I am!

NETTIE

(*Out of shot*) I was expecting Victor Rodney's son. Has he not come?

MRS TRINGSBY

He's standing outside the door, my dear.

NETTIE

Well, why doesn't he come in?

RODERICK *goes in.*

INT. NETTIE'S ROOM. DAY

NETTIE *sitting with needlework, her back to the window.*

RODERICK

Cousin Nettie.

MRS TRINGSBY

I shall be just downstairs. (*She points to a bell.*) Just downstairs.

NETTIE

Thank you, Mrs Tringsby.

MRS TRINGSBY *goes.* NETTIE *continues with her needlework. He watches her.*

I expect you would never have the patience to do this?

RODERICK

No, I expect not.

NETTIE

But you must *have* patience – to have come such a long journey. It's such a long way to here.

RODERICK

Oh, not so very long – not from where I came from.

NETTIE

I thought it was too far for anybody to come.

He sits.

So you remembered me. Even though you have never met me? Are you called Victor too?

RODERICK

No. Roderick.

NETTIE

Then I shall call you Roderick. I'm so glad you're not called Victor.

RODERICK

I shall call my son, whenever I have one, Francis.

NETTIE

Oh, he would be so pleased. What a pity he's dead.

RODERICK

It's because he's dead that I've come. I hope my coming doesn't upset you?

NETTIE

I hope I shan't upset you. I believe I am very odd. And you must not tell me I'm not – or I shall begin to wonder.

RODERICK

Do you know Cousin Francis left Mount Morris to me?

NETTIE

Mount Morris, poor unfortunate house, poor thing! So there it is, after all this time, and here I am!

RODERICK

I wanted to ask –

NETTIE

No, you must not ask me, no! I cannot come back. I told him again and again, and I told them – now I am telling you. Everywhere is better without me. I cannot come back.

Silence.

Oh, I wish you could have seen him when he was a young man. Head and shoulders above all the rest of them. And there could have been a different story. There could. But there wasn't and in the end he had to go out looking for a son.

The MAID *comes in with tray.*

MAID

There, dear.

NETTIE

Thank you, Hilda.

MAID

Sandwiches for the gentleman.

She goes.

NETTIE

Will you have a sandwich?

RODERICK *takes one.*

RODERICK

Cousin Nettie, I have decided that I want to live at Mount Morris. I'm not asking you to come back. All I'm saying is, I shall consider the house as much yours as mine.

NETTIE

Day after day at Mount Morris was sinking further down a well. It became too much for me – but how could I say so? I could not help seeing what was the matter – what he had wanted me to be was his wife. I tried this, that and the other, till the result was that I fell into such a terrible melancholy that I only had to think of anything for it to go wrong. Nature hated us. Once the fields noticed me with him, the harvests began to fail. So I took to going nowhere but up and down stairs, till I met my own ghost.

EXT. MOUNT MORRIS, IRELAND. EVENING

The house is large. Two girls standing on the steps. A pony and trap comes down the drive and stops. DONOVAN *helps* STELLA *from the trap. The two girls take Stella's cases. They all go in to the house.*

INT. MOUNT MORRIS: LIBRARY. EVENING

A large dark picture. White cards stuck around the inside frame.

STELLA *walks forward and peers at the cards. She reads: Locks and Hinges, my method of oiling . . . Live mice caught in traps to be drowned not dropped in kitchen fire . . . In case of blocked gutters . . . in case of parachutists . . . in case of my death . . .*

STELLA *turns away. A fire blazing in a distant marble fireplace. She looks out of the window.*

DONOVAN *comes into the room with an oil lamp. He turns the wick high. The globe wells up with yellow light.* MARY DONOVAN *(aged nineteen) enters with another lamp. The two globes are reflected in the window panes.*

DONOVAN

This has been a bare sort of time for us, ma'am, with neither master – and it's a poor welcome for you, I fear, but indeed you're welcome.

STELLA

Thank you.

DONOVAN

We killed a little chicken for your supper.

STELLA

Oh, how nice.

DONOVAN

Will you see your room? (*To* MARY)
Are there candles?

MARY

There are two candles above.

EXT. MOUNT MORRIS. NIGHT

River flowing.
Moonlight reflected in rows of windows.
STELLA*'s figure tiny in an upper window.*

INT. MOUNT MORRIS: STELLA'S BEDROOM. MORNING

She draws the curtains swiftly, looks out. A brilliant morning. Swans on the river.

INT. MOUNT MORRIS: HALL. MORNING

STELLA *and* DONOVAN *meeting.*

DONOVAN
They'll be here from the surveyors in about half an hour, ma'am.

STELLA
Oh, right. Donovan, is there a boat? My son wants to know if there is a boat.

DONOVAN
Ah, well now, there was a boat until the master sank her. He had the boys out one morning loading rock into her until she went down.

STELLA
But why did he do that?

DONOVAN
Mr Robertson's advice. I think he thought the Germans might be landing here and that they'd fancy the use of a boat.

CALDERDALE
COLLEGE LIBRARY
HALIFAX

STELLA

Mr Robertson?

DONOVAN

Some name of that sort. He came from over. Whether he was a Mister or a Captain we never made out.

STELLA

What did he look like?

DONOVAN

He had a narrow sort of look about him, added to which he had a sort of discord between his two eyes.

INT. MOUNT MORRIS: LIBRARY. NIGHT

STELLA *lifting a photograph from a magazine stuck in a frame from a corner of the room: a liner going down in a blaze with all the lights on. Title:* NEARER MY GOD TO THEE: THE TITANIC: 1912.

INT. MOUNT MORRIS: BEDROOM. NIGHT

STELLA *lying in bed, eyes open. Half a candle burning. It goes out.*

EXT. MOUNT MORRIS: WOODS. DAY

STELLA *walking along path through woods. She stops. On the path is the body of a big bird, dead. She stares at it.*

INT. MOUNT MORRIS: LIBRARY. EVENING

STELLA *trying to open drawers in the library. They are locked.*

INT. MOUNT MORRIS: DRAWING ROOM. NIGHT

She moves about the room, catching her reflection in mirrors and window panes. She stops by a piano and strikes a chord.

INT. MOUNT MORRIS: BEDROOM. NIGHT

A candle guttering. It goes out.

EXT. MOUNT MORRIS: RIVER. DAY

Morning. STELLA *standing by the flowing river, looking into it. A call. She looks up.* DONOVAN *is standing on a parapet. His daughter,* HANNAH, *(aged twenty) stands next to him. She is beautiful. He shapes both his hands into a megaphone.*

DONOVAN

Montgomery's through!
STELLA *makes a gesture of not hearing.* DONOVAN *calls again.*
Montgomery's through! Victory!
STELLA *walks quickly to the house. She begins to walk up a slope towards the parapet.*

STELLA

Montgomery?

DONOVAN

A terrible victory! Victory in a day!
She stumbles up the slope. He reaches for her hand, grips it.
Come up with you, ma'am.
He pulls her up to him.
The day's famous.

HANNAH

It's a beautiful day, in any event.

STELLA *looks at her.* HANNAH *stands quietly in the sunshine 'indifferent as a wand'.*

INT. EUSTON STATION: PLATFORM. NIGHT

Train arriving. Doors burst open.

STELLA *gets off the train, walks along the platform.*

Through surging crowds she sees ROBERT, *stock still under a light, looking.*

She goes on. The crowd. She looks for ROBERT. *He is gone.*

Suddenly he is at her side, kissing her, taking her case.

ROBERT

What a needle in a bundle of hay. Let's get out of this.

He steers her towards the arches.

STELLA

Why this way?

ROBERT

I have a car. With a driver.

STELLA

Oh. Wonderful.

ROBERT

One snag. Ernestine's in it.

STELLA

Oh no! Why?

ROBERT

She's up for the day. We're just dropping her off at a friend. That's all. Five minutes. Do you love me?

STELLA

Why?

ROBERT

Then nothing matters.

EXT. EUSTON STATION: FORECOURT. NIGHT

ROBERT *shines torch on number plates. It is raining. He bangs on a window. A driver jumps out, opens door, they get in.*

INT. CAR. NIGHT

The car is capacious. Jump seats in the back. A glass partition.

ERNESTINE

Mrs Rodney! You must be dead.

STELLA

Not quite.

ERNESTINE

How was the Emerald Isle? Plenty of eggs and bacon?

STELLA

It was rather strange that they had no blackout.

ERNESTINE

Do they actually *know* there's a war on?

ROBERT

Yes. Because they know they're not in it.
The car moves off.
ROBERT *sits facing the women. He tucks a rug over* STELLA*'s knees.*
Here.
ERNESTINE *laughs.*

ERNESTINE

So the age of chivalry is not yet dead! Robert, the driver does know we're going to Earls Court, I take it?

ROBERT

Of course.

ERNESTINE

You told him?

ROBERT

I told him.

ERNESTINE

I didn't hear you tell him. You seemed so fussed at Euston Station. However . . .

STELLA *lies back and closes her eyes.*

ERNESTINE *snaps her handbag open and searches about in it.*

Oh God!

STELLA *opens her eyes.*

STELLA

Have you lost something?

ERNESTINE

I hope to heaven I haven't! I thought you were asleep.

ROBERT

So did I. What were you doing? Thinking?

STELLA

No . . . just . . .

ERNESTINE

It must be somewhere! I'm sure I put it in my handbag this morning. If I didn't I should be shot! Ah! Got it! Scoundrel! Thank heaven for that!

ROBERT

Thinking what?

ERNESTINE

What?

ROBERT

I was asking Stella what she was thinking.

STELLA

I'm so glad you found it.

ERNESTINE

Why should she tell you? I really don't know why she's not allowed to think in peace. Ask no questions and you'll be told no lies. Where are we? Has anybody any idea? Hey! It's Earls Court! Driver!

ROBERT

He knows.

EXT. EARLS COURT. NIGHT

ERNESTINE *gets out of the car.* ROBERT *kisses her, gets back in. The car drives off.*

INT. CAR. NIGHT

ROBERT *sitting next to* STELLA.

STELLA

(*Quickly*) What do you think she lost?

ROBERT

Mmmnn?

STELLA

And then found? In her handbag?

ROBERT

I haven't the foggiest idea.

STELLA

Whatever it was what a relief she found it. You've never told me –

ROBERT

What?

STELLA

You've never told me what she was like when she was young –

He kisses her. She is tense. He withdraws, regards her. As the car moves through the traffic (all cars with dimmed lights) it is only the occasional traffic light that illumines their faces.

I'm sorry. I can't . . . just be alone with you all at once. It was a shock seeing you at Euston – it's a shock – I'm just thrown – I'll be all right – Let me . . .

Pause.

ROBERT

I know you've been all by yourself in that house, but all the same . . . I feel jealous, as though somehow you've been with some sort of enemy of mine – or rival. So far the best thing has been touching your coat. I know where I am with your coat. It's just the same.

STELLA

You have no enemy anywhere in me!

ROBERT

Why should you have to say that?

STELLA

My darling, who could like to feel less welcome than her own coat?

ROBERT

But I want to welcome you. Totally. You haven't let me.

STELLA

Can you give me a cigarette?
He gives her a cigarette, lights a match, the match goes out. He strikes another one, lights her cigarette.
The car enters a dark section of the street. Her voice:
Two months ago, nearly two months ago, somebody came to me with a story about you. They said you were passing information to the enemy.
Silence.

ROBERT

I what?

STELLA

They said you were passing information to the enemy. I didn't . . . I didn't know what to think.
Silence.

ROBERT

What an extraordinary woman you are.

STELLA

Why? What would an ordinary woman . . . have thought? What would an ordinary woman have done?

ROBERT

Well, I don't know really. What did you do?

STELLA

Nothing. It's not true, is it?

ROBERT

Two months ago . . . two *months*? There's certainly nothing like thinking a thing over. Or did it happen to simply slip your mind until tonight? Why didn't you just

come and ask me then? What would have been wrong with that? Or was that too simple?
Traffic lights on their faces.
That's what beats me.
Pause.
Who *was* this?

STELLA

A man called Harrison.

ROBERT

A man called Harrison.

STELLA

It isn't true, is it?

ROBERT

It can't be true that you're asking me the question. What do you want me to say? There's nothing *to* say! The whole thing's so completely unreal to me I can't believe it isn't as unreal to you. It must be.

STELLA

Yes, it is. But –

ROBERT

What you're asking me isn't the point – it's immaterial, crazy, out of a thriller. Am I passing information to the enemy? No, of course not! How could I be, why should I? What do you take me for? What *do* you take me for? What do I take you for? How well you've acted with me for the last two months. How could you – ? I ask you again. Why didn't you come to me two months ago and tell me then?

STELLA

He said it would be dangerous to you to tell you.

ROBERT

What he says, then, cuts a good deal of ice with you?
Pause.
In fact you acted on the assumption that it was true.

STELLA

I didn't act! I didn't know what to do. I loved you.

ROBERT

How strange that word sounds.

STELLA

Oh my darling – for God's sake – this is breaking my heart –

ROBERT

Is it? Am I? Or are you just saying so? How do you expect me to know what's true? You may have had another lover all this time for all I know. I'm not sure I wouldn't have preferred that. This is so . . . So you've been watching me for two months? You're two months gone with this. And I didn't see it. I must be going blind.

STELLA

I . . . loved you . . .

ROBERT

No. It's the appearance of love you keep up so beautifully.

STELLA

(*Closing her eyes*) No. No.
Silence. She suddenly laughs.
Well, I suppose I owe you an apology.

ROBERT

What? Oh . . . yes . . . I suppose you do.

STELLA

I'm . . . shocked too, you know. Until I heard my own words and heard you hear them, I really had no idea how horrible . . . forgive me.
The car goes on.
Robert?

ROBERT

Yes. I'm listening to you.

STELLA

Say something.

ROBERT

You don't seem to have shown any great patriotic fervour.

STELLA

No.
She opens the window and breathes deeply.

ROBERT

What is it?

STELLA

I think I'm weak with hunger.

ROBERT

Yes, that's what it probably is. We'll get a sandwich somewhere.

STELLA

Will we? Do you want to?

ROBERT

Oh yes. I've had quite a day too as days go. I need a drink. We're both a bit light-headed. A drink will sober us down.

INT. HOTEL LOUNGE. NIGHT

ROBERT *and* STELLA *at a table with drinks and sandwiches. In the background continual movement of foreign officers.*

ROBERT

Must have been strange . . . Ireland?

STELLA

Yes. It was the light as much as anything else.

ROBERT

Mmn.

STELLA

Dublin was a blaze of light – as the ship came in. It was dazzling . . . frightening. And at the house – there were oil lamps in the windows – you know – naked windows. It was strange, yes.
They drink.
One night I took a lamp and went into the drawing room. I walked up and down it and I imagined Roderick's wife in it one day. Why not, after all? Roderick's wife . . . but there was a picture of the *Titanic* hanging crooked in a corner –

ROBERT

Stella –

STELLA

Yes?

ROBERT

Talking of that, why shouldn't we marry?

STELLA

Talking of the *Titanic*?

CALDERDALE
COLLEGE LIBRARY
HALIFAX

ROBERT

No, talking of Roderick. If anyone is to marry, why not us?

STELLA

You and me?

ROBERT

Yes. Why not?
She looks at him.

STELLA

We've got in the way of not marrying, I suppose.

ROBERT

Yes, but why not?
She does not answer.
Why not? You know it's really quite simple. The reason that I want to marry you is that I want to marry you. I made up my mind when you were in Ireland. The fact is I can't bear you out of my sight.

STELLA

But I hardly ever am.

ROBERT

I'm not so sure as I used to be about that.

STELLA

You think I run into trouble?

ROBERT

I think you do a bit, yes.

STELLA

You think I need looking after?

ROBERT

Your friend what's-his-name must have thought so.

STELLA

Why do you call him what's-his-name? His name is Harrison. It's an easy name to remember.

ROBERT

Harrison. But what if I need looking after too? Do you think that perhaps you and I have never quite been our ages?

STELLA

I thought it had all been perfect.

ROBERT

Yes, it all seemed perfect. But there must have been a catch in it somewhere. We must have been about due to take this knock.

They stare at each other.

There's only one solution. Marry me. It's not such a new idea. It's not such a wild idea.

STELLA

You've made it sound wild. You're contradicting yourself. First you say you made up your mind when I was in Ireland – then you say you feel forced to ask me because of what I said in the car – because it suddenly seems necessary for you to keep me under your eye – also – and I understand all of this – that I owe some . . . balm to your offended honour. Well, that's how you make it sound – that the very least I can do is marry you, to prove to you I'm convinced anything more I might possibly hear about you can't be true. So any reasons I may have of my *own* – to hesitate – go by the board. Don't you see?

ROBERT

Look, I was clear enough. Let's get this straight. The fact that I want to marry you has nothing to do with what you said in the car. If Ernie hadn't been sitting waiting I'd have asked you the moment I saw you on the platform. I'm not saying that what happened later didn't have an effect on me. Of course it did – it made me more certain it was time we married. The idea of anyone who likes coming along and frightening you is appalling. Yes, I was hurt too – how could I hide that? How could I not be? But – more to the point – for a moment the whole of our love seemed futile if I couldn't keep you . . . from that fantastic thing.

STELLA

Yes, it was fantastic.

ROBERT

But you were frightened.

STELLA

Yes.

ROBERT

Yes. For me – but also of me – a little?

STELLA

It was simply . . .

ROBERT

Do you love me?

STELLA

We're keeping the waiter waiting.

ROBERT *looks down and sees a bill on the plate on the table.*

Not just anybody can frighten me, you know. I wish you'd find out who Harrison is.

ROBERT

Is he anybody?

INT. THE FLAT. DAY

STELLA *lifting the phone.*

STELLA

Hello?

ROBERT

(*Voice over*) Darling, it's me. I'm sorry, dammit, I can't make tonight. I have to go down to Holme Dene. A family convocation. Red alert. My mother has had an offer for the house. Thrown them completely. I have to go. What will you do?

STELLA

Oh – I'll have a quiet night.

ROBERT

I'll ring you tomorrow.
The phone cuts off. She turns. HARRISON *is in the room.*

EXT. REGENT STREET. NIGHT

HARRISON *walking with* STELLA. *They wear raincoats. He takes her elbow as they cross into a side street.*

HARRISON

Here we are. This is it. Down these steps. Careful.
They go down into a basement. A dim sign on the door. CAFÉ OPEN. *They go in.*

INT. BASEMENT CAFÉ. NIGHT

They enter the café. It is a bar/grill. People seated along the counter. There are also tables.
HARRISON *takes* STELLA *to a table for two.*

HARRISON

(*Handing menu*) Here you are.

STELLA

I'm thirsty. I'd love some lager.

HARRISON

Yes, absolutely.
He waves to a WAITRESS.
Two lagers please. (*To* STELLA) And what about food? See anything you like? Cold cuts and salad? Fish? Wait, I'll tell you what. Let's see if they can do something . . . different. After all, this is an occasion – for me anyway.
He goes to the bar and talks to the MANAGERESS. *The* WAITRESS *brings the lagers to the table.* STELLA *sips.* HARRISON *returns, sits, winks.*
Just the job. Mission accomplished.

STELLA

What is it?

HARRISON

A secret.

STELLA

I'm not very hungry.

HARRISON

Well . . . no worry . . . it's just very nice for me . . . to be your escort . . . Cheers.

STELLA

Cheers.
They drink.

HARRISON

Mind you, I still have to scold you, I'm afraid.

STELLA

Oh? Why?

HARRISON

You've done what I told you not to do.

STELLA

What's that?

HARRISON

You've been naughty.

STELLA

Really?

HARRISON

Yes, really. Also . . . rash. One of these days you'll be getting some of us into trouble. Don't look blank – you know very well what you've done.
She drinks.
You tipped him off. Didn't you? Come on. Admit it.
She looks at him.
I mean if I've got it wrong, you can always tell me to go to hell. Why don't you tell me to go to hell?

STELLA

Perhaps you're growing on me.
HARRISON *drinks.*

HARRISON

You know, you're not as bright as I thought.

STELLA

Oh?

HARRISON

No. When I told you, at the very beginning, that I should know if you tipped him off, you really should have believed me. You see, I not only know that you have, but I can

tell you when. I can tell you the very day, or rather the very night.
WAITRESS *to table.*

WAITRESS

Two lobster salad.

HARRISON

Lovely.
The WAITRESS *puts the plates down on the table and goes.*
This was my secret. My innocent secret.

STELLA

There's no such thing as an innocent secret.

HARRISON

Isn't there? But you like lobster, I hope?

STELLA

Oh, yes. I like it very much.

HARRISON

I'm glad. Looks fresh, doesn't it?

STELLA

It does . . . look fresh.
They begin to eat.
What makes you think you can tell me the day or the night?

HARRISON

Because, from the morning after, he altered his course. Behaved in fact exactly, and to the letter, the way I told you he would behave the moment he knew there was someone on his tracks. That's what I said he'd do and that's what he's done. So I know you told him.

STELLA

When?

HARRISON

The night you got back from Ireland.

STELLA

Well . . .

She takes out her powder compact, begins to powder her nose, looks in the mirror.

Well . . .

LOUIE *comes into the café. She sits at the bar, suddenly sees* HARRISON, *stares at him, half smiles.* STELLA *sees her in the mirror.*

Someone has recognized you.

HARRISON

What?

STELLA

A friend of yours.

HARRISON

Don't be silly.

STELLA

At the bar.

HARRISON *looks round.* LOUIE *smiles at him. He turns back to the table.*

A dog wanders among the tables, leash trailing.

HARRISON

What you've done is this – you've put us all on the spot. You see? Thanks to you, our friend has pretty well dished himself. The only case for leaving him loose was the chance he would lead us on to something bigger. Now that's out. So the case for leaving him loose falls down. That's what it's up to me to report.

STELLA

So will you?

HARRISON

I've got myself to think of too, you know. And the country.

STELLA

So far, who besides you knows this?
He looks at her.

HARRISON

Only I know. It still has to go up –

STELLA

And you wouldn't be telling me this if it had . . . *gone* up? Is that right?
The dog nuzzles STELLA*'s leg.* HARRISON *kicks at it.*

HARRISON

Scram!

STELLA

It's not doing any harm.

HARRISON

It's bothering you.

STELLA

It won't bite. I wish it would. What were we saying?

HARRISON

You know what we were saying.

STELLA

I know what you were about to say, yes. That at last, now, it really is up to me. That I either buy out Robert for a bit longer . . . or –

HARRISON *claps his hand down on hers sharply.* LOUIE *is at the table.*

LOUIE

Excuse me. I'm just after my dog. Come along, come on Spot, bad boy. Bothering people!
She looks at HARRISON.
Hello. I haven't seen you in the park for ages.
HARRISON *picks up the leash and hands it to her.*

HARRISON

I'm never there.

LOUIE

Well, you must have been there once. I saw you there. Fancy seeing you here! (*To* STELLA) Excuse me interrupting, it's on account of Spot. Bad boy.

STELLA

You're not interrupting. Why do you call your dog Spot? He hasn't got any.

LOUIE

He's my friend's dog actually. I was going to meet her in this café. But I think I've come to the wrong place, I mean the wrong café –

HARRISON

Well, you'd better buzz off home. And take your dog.

LOUIE

He's taken quite a fancy to you, hasn't he? They always say a dog knows . . .

STELLA

Why don't you sit down?
LOUIE *glances at* HARRISON.

CALDERDALE
COLLEGE LIBRARY
HALIFAX

LOUIE

Oh, I –

STELLA

For a minute.

LOUIE *brings a chair from the next table and sits.*

LOUIE

I don't think I should, really. For one thing, you were talking.

STELLA

Oh, we were only deciding something.

LOUIE *looks round the café.*

LOUIE

My friend's not here. I wish I knew where we were.

STELLA

I've no idea where we are! (*To* HARRISON) Where are we? (*To* LOUIE) Do tell me your name. I'm Mrs Rodney.

LOUIE

I'm Mrs Lewis.

STELLA

Are you?

LOUIE

Yes. I've got a husband in India – well, somewhere like that. (*She looks at* HARRISON.) To think of you remembering me . . .

STELLA

You're not old friends then?

LOUIE

Oh, no. We just fell into conversation at a band concert in the park. Didn't we? Weeks ago.

HARRISON *ignores her.*

HARRISON

(*To* STELLA, *viciously*) Are you off your head? Do you think we've got all night?

STELLA

Yes, I thought we had.
LOUIE *looks at them.*

LOUIE

(*Violently*) How can you talk to her like that? How can you go out with him? Why does he talk to you like that? People to be friendly, that's what the war's for, isn't it?

STELLA

I'm sorry.
She picks up Louie's gloves from the floor and gives them to her.
You mustn't mind him. You mustn't blame him. It's been my fault. He's in trouble too. This evening was to have been a celebration, the first of many more evenings. It may still be the first of many more evenings, but what will they be worth? I don't know.
LOUIE *stands.*

LOUIE

Well, I'll be off. Goodnight.

STELLA

Say goodnight to him.

LOUIE

I don't know his name.

STELLA

Harrison. You must congratulate me before you go. I've good news, I think.

LOUIE

You have?

STELLA

Yes. A friend is out of danger.

HARRISON*'s hand moves abruptly to his eye. The table jolts. He rubs his eye, puts his cigarette out in the ashtray.*

HARRISON

Why don't you two both go along together?

STELLA *stares at him.*

Didn't you hear what I said? You two had better both be getting along.

STELLA

But . . .

HARRISON

What?

STELLA

But . . . we don't know where we are . . .

HARRISON

Turn right, first left and you're in Regent Street.

STELLA

I don't understand. What has been decided? I thought we . . . What have you decided? What are you going to do?

HARRISON

Pay the bill.

INT. HOLME DENE: LOUNGE. NIGHT

MRS KELWAY *and* ERNESTINE *sitting.* ROBERT *standing, pacing about, sometimes coming to rest on the hearth rug. He paces, stops.*

ROBERT

Let's sum up: (a) we don't know if we want to sell (b) if we do, how much more than the offer do we hope to get? (c) again, if we do sell, where are you both to go?

MRS KELWAY

I am afraid it is not so simple as that.

ERNESTINE

Muttikins feels there must be something behind the offer.

ROBERT

What's behind the offer is that someone wants to buy the house.

ERNESTINE

Who can want to buy a house they haven't seen?

ROBERT

How do you know they haven't seen it?

ERNESTINE

Well, no one has been to the door!

ROBERT

You can see the house from a little way down the drive.

MRS KELWAY

We do not care for people coming down the drive.

ERNESTINE

Why can't they come to the door and openly ring the bell? Creeping and spying about . . .

MRS KELWAY

No one is going to rush us. We did not ask these people to buy the house.

ROBERT

But we left 'For Sale' on the agent's books for years.

MRS KELWAY

Nevertheless, this is our home.

ROBERT

In that case – we turn 'em down.

MRS KELWAY

But it *is* too large.

ROBERT

In that case – we jack 'em up.

MRS KELWAY

I am afraid it is not so simple as that.
Pause.

ERNESTINE

You talk, Robert, as though this was just a business transaction.

MRS KELWAY

It always has been too large. And too expensive. Your father made a mistake. One of many.

ROBERT

Could you actually be happy in something smaller?

MRS KELWAY

It is not a question of happiness. It is a question of the future. That is for you and Ernestine. I have had my life and I hope I have done my best. But you must not expect me to be with you for long.

ERNESTINE

Muttikins! Don't say such dreadful things!

MRS KELWAY

You talk as though you expected not to die yourself. We shall –

The telephone rings in the hall.

ROBERT *starts violently, stops walking.*

ERNESTINE *jumps up and goes into the hall.*

ERNESTINE

It'll be for me!

ROBERT *remains still as* ERNESTINE*'s voice is heard.*

Yes, yes! Of course! Nine thirty. But can we all get in . . . Oh, yes I'm all for it . . . yes, yes – all hands on deck!

She returns.

Oh, it has been a day! One thing after another.

MRS KELWAY

Ernestine has not been able to take her hat off.

ERNESTINE

Well, ought we to sell or not?

ROBERT

Do we want to?

ERNESTINE

One can't always be thinking of what one wants.

MRS KELWAY

I have never thought of what I wanted. Don't forget that this house is to be left to you both jointly. If you do not care for that you had better say so.

ERNESTINE

Of course we care! How can I ever forget this is my home?

ROBERT

How can I?

MRS KELWAY *looks at* ROBERT.

MRS KELWAY

And so, what is your advice?

Pause.

ROBERT

Sell.

ERNESTINE *laughs.*

MRS KELWAY

Robert does not remember anything about his life.

ROBERT *regards her coldly.*

ROBERT

There you are quite wrong . . . Muttikins.

She looks at him and then at ERNESTINE.

MRS KELWAY

He talks like a man.

Silence.

A sound from the hall.

ROBERT

Who's there?

He goes to the door. ANNE *comes down the stairs and into the room.*

ANNE

Me, Uncle Robert.

ERNESTINE

Anne!

ANNE

Oh, Auntie Ernie, please.

ERNESTINE

Both of you ought to be sound asleep.

ANNE

Peter is.

ERNESTINE

Granny doesn't like people creeping about in the middle of the night.

ANNE

I know, but –

ERNESTINE

Don't say 'I know' to Granny.

ROBERT *scoops* ANNE *up and sits her on the arm of an armchair, in which he sits.*

Robert, you encourage her.

ROBERT

No, she encourages me.

He rocks ANNE *to and fro by her belt.*

But I think you might have cooked up something cleverer? Why couldn't you be walking in your sleep?

ANNE

Because I'm awake. Can you stay here tonight?

ROBERT

No. Got anything to tell me?

ANNE

I was top at mental arithmetic.

ERNESTINE

You can tell Uncle Robert all about that next time –

ROBERT

No, really, Ernie.

ERNESTINE

Well then, a moment. Only a moment, mind.

ANNE

(*To* ROBERT) How many moments are there? How long, compared to a minute, is a moment?

ROBERT

That depends on –
Telephone.
ROBERT *jumps.* ANNE *falls off the chair.*

MRS KELWAY

The telephone is never for anybody but Ernestine. What is the matter, Robert? Are you expecting a call?

ERNESTINE

If it's for you, do answer it.

MRS KELWAY

Knocking the child off the chair . . . Oh, need we have all that ringing? Will, someone answer it?

ANNE

I will.
She runs into the hall.

ERNESTINE

Anne, no!
ROBERT *stands up.*
Oh, I'll answer it.

MRS KELWAY

Is it for Robert?

ERNESTINE

Does anyone know you're here?

ROBERT

If it's for me, say I'm on my way back to London, will you?

ANNE

But you're here.

The telephone stops.

ERNESTINE

There – you see! If it should turn out to be important, I shall always blame myself. Now, Anne – to bed.

ANNE *flings her arms around* ROBERT. *He stoops, presses her cheek to his.*

ANNE

Are you going to London?

ROBERT

Yes.

ANNE

You're always going away. Always.

ROBERT

You're giving me a crick in my back. You must grow taller.

ANNE

Just one more.

She pulls his head down and gently butts her forehead against his.

INT. STELLA'S FLAT: BEDROOM. 2 A.M.

Light from the electric fire.

STELLA *is sitting in the bed.* ROBERT *is sitting at the foot of the bed. They are both naked.*

Silence.

ROBERT

And if I am? If that is what I am doing?
Silence.
Because it has been that, all the time.
Silence.

STELLA

Why?

ROBERT

Oh . . . we should have to try to understand each other all over again. It's too late now.

STELLA

Too late in the night?
Pause.

ROBERT

Too late.

STELLA

Why are you against this country?

ROBERT

Country?

STELLA

Yes.

ROBERT

There are no countries. Nothing but names. What sort of country do you think exists outside this room? Exhausted shadows, dragging themselves to fight. How long can they drag the fight out? We've come out on the far side of that.

STELLA

We?

ROBERT

We . . . who are ready for the next thing.

STELLA

What is it? What is the next thing?

ROBERT

The next thing . . . is something . . . on an altogether different scale. It's . . . sight in *action*. When I *act* I see.
Pause.
Do you think I'm a traitor? All that language is dead currency. It means nothing. What it once meant is gone.
Pause.
Are you against me?

STELLA

You're the one who's against. But not this country, you say? Then what are you against?

ROBERT

The racket.

STELLA

What racket?

ROBERT

Freedom. Freedom to be what? Muddled, mediocre, damned. Look at your free people. Mice let loose in the middle of the Sahara. It's insupportable. Tell a man he's free – you know what that does to him? It sends him scuttling back into the womb. Look at it. Look at your mass of 'free' suckers – look at your 'democracy' – kidded along from the cradle to the grave. Do you think there's a single man of *mind* who doesn't know *he* only begins where his 'freedom' stops? Freedom is just a slave's yammer. One in a thousand may have what it takes to be free – if so, he has what it takes to be something better. And he knows it. Who would want to be free when he could be strong? We must be strong. There must be law.

STELLA

But you break the law.

ROBERT

No. Not the real law, not the true law.
He stands, walks silently to the window, pulls the curtains. Moonlight. His silhouette at the window. He stands still.

STELLA

Come back.
He turns, goes back to the bed, sits, not touching.

ROBERT

Do you feel I've been apart from you in this? I haven't. There's been you and me in everything I've done.

STELLA

Why didn't you . . . talk to me?

ROBERT

I couldn't involve you. How could I? And how was I to tell you? How?

STELLA

You could have . . . just let me know.

ROBERT

Sometimes I thought I had. There were times it seemed impossible you didn't know. I found myself waiting for you to speak. When you didn't I thought you had decided silence was better – and I thought, yes, silence is better. But I didn't know that you didn't know – until you asked me.
She suddenly sobs.

STELLA

Oh, why did you? What made you have to? Such ideas to have . . . Why?

ROBERT

I didn't choose them. They marked me out. They're not mine. I'm theirs. Haven't I a right to my own side?
He leans towards her and takes her hand.
It is enough to have been in action once on the wrong side. You don't know the disgust – of Dunkirk. An army of freedom queuing up to be taken off by pleasure boats. That was the end of *that* war. What was left? The scum – the Dunkirk wounded.

STELLA

I never knew you before then . . . before you were wounded.

ROBERT

I was born wounded. My father's son. Dunkirk was waiting there in us. What a race! A class without a middle. A race without a country. Never earthed in. Thousands and thousands of us – breeding and breeding – breeding what?
Pause.

STELLA

Were you never frightened – to do what you were doing?

ROBERT

The opposite. It undid fear. It bred my father out of me. It gave me a new heredity. I was living. I was under orders.

STELLA

So you're with the enemy.

ROBERT

They're facing us with what has got to be the conclusion. They may not last. But it will.

STELLA

It's not just that they're the enemy – but that they're horrible, unthinkable, grotesque.

ROBERT

In birth anything is grotesque. But they've started something. You may not like it but it's the beginning of a new world.

STELLA

Roderick may be killed.
Silence.
Roderick may be killed.
He does not speak.
I have *not* been in what you've done. The more I understand it the more I hate it. I hate it.
She stands, puts on gown, goes to door, goes out of bedroom, closes door.

INT. SITTING ROOM. NIGHT

Darkness. She switches on a lamp. She walks to the mantelpiece. She looks at ROBERT*'s photograph. She turns the photograph to the wall.*
She trembles, holds on to the shelf, tries to call 'Robert' but has no voice.
The bedroom door opens. ROBERT *in dressing-gown.*

ROBERT

Yes?
She looks at him.
You called me?
They fall into each other's arms. He holds her to him. The photograph of ROBERT *falls off the mantelshelf on to the floor.*

STELLA

I should never have let you come here. This will be the first place they –

ROBERT

Last night at Holme Dene I was in terror of never seeing you again. I knew I was in danger but I'd never pictured arrest before. I suddenly did. What a place to be taken in! Theirs to be the last faces I saw! My mother had been waiting for this. She wished it! It would be she who had got me into this trap, so that I should never see you again. It never suited her that I should be a man.
He lights a cigarette, sits on the sofa.
I wonder how they got on to me? I wonder what I did – what I didn't think of? I was so careful. It had become second nature.
She sits.

STELLA

If I had slept with Harrison, could he have . . . saved you?

ROBERT

What, did he say so? Naturally he would. You didn't try?

STELLA

I thought I would, last night. But he sent me home.

ROBERT

You left it pretty late.

STELLA

I left it late, yes.

ROBERT

He sounds crazy. What a chance to take. What was to stop you turning him in? It would have been the end of him.

STELLA

It would have been the end of you too.
She takes a cigarette. He lights it.
What are you then? A revolutionary? No, a counter-revolutionary? What are you exactly? You know, for

CALDERDALE
COLLEGE LIBRARY
HALIFAX

somebody doing something so definite, you talk so vaguely. Wildness and images. It's as though you haven't formulated . . . everything in your mind.

ROBERT

I've never talked about it before.

STELLA

Not even to your . . . friends?

ROBERT

You think we meet to swap ideas?
Pause.

STELLA

Something's missing. You are out for the enemy to win because you think they have something. What?

ROBERT

They have something. This war's just so much bloody quibbling about a thing that's pre-decided. Either side's winning would stop the war – only their side's winning would stop the quibbling. I want order. I want shape. I want discipline. I want the cackle cut. What have I still not said?
They sit.

STELLA

I wish we could sleep.

ROBERT

I must dress.

STELLA

Going? But there might be someone outside the door?

ROBERT

Yes. There has been a step.

STELLA

When? I didn't hear. And if it had been his step I should have heard it. I should have known it before I heard it.
She goes towards the window.

ROBERT

Don't touch the curtain!
She stops.

STELLA

I want to. I want to say:
'Yes, he's here – we're here together, he's with me, I love him!'
ROBERT *goes into the bedroom and begins to dress. They speak through the open door.*
I could let you out the back.

ROBERT

If there's somebody at the front there'll be someone at the back.

STELLA

That could depend on whether the somebody at the front is Harrison or not.

ROBERT

Why?

STELLA

He's in love. He could be watching the house for his own reasons. People torment themselves.

ROBERT

He's still what he is.

STELLA

You were mad to come here.
ROBERT *comes out of the bedroom, dressed, goes to her.*

ROBERT

I had to hold you in my arms . . . once more. And I had to tell you. I came here to tell you but I had to hold you in my arms first. I had to love you first and then tell you. I wonder . . . would we ever have spoken if we hadn't known this was goodbye?

STELLA

(*Dully*) This is goodbye.

ROBERT

Isn't there a way out on to the roof?

STELLA

Yes, yes . . . the skylight . . . you know it . . . but there could be somebody there . . . there could be somebody on the roof.

ROBERT

There's one great thing about a roof. There's one sure way off it.
They stand.

STELLA

It's steep. I wish you hadn't got your stiff knee.

ROBERT

I wish I hadn't got my stiff knee. We've never danced . . . have we?
Silence.
I'll go by the roof. Come on.
He goes to the door. She follows.

INT. LANDING. NIGHT

The ladder to the skylight down. ROBERT *goes up it, pushes the skylight. It opens. He secures it. He comes down the ladder, kisses her.*

ROBERT

Take care of yourself.
He goes up the ladder, stops.
Now, turn off the light, get back into the flat and shut the door.
The light goes out.

STELLA'S VOICE

Goodnight.

EXT. FRONT OF THE HOUSE. NIGHT

A figure standing.

EXT. BACK OF THE HOUSE. NIGHT

A figure standing.
A moving figure on the roof.

EXT. FRONT OF THE HOUSE. NIGHT

Figure on the roof.

EXT. BACK OF THE HOUSE. NIGHT

Roof empty. A man running. A thud.

CLICK OF A CAMERA

Photograph of ROBERT, *spreadeagled in basement, still.*

EXT. LONDON STREET. NIGHT

Fifteen months later. An air raid taking place. Bombs. Gunfire. Searchlights, etc.
HARRISON *standing in street looking up at block of flats in Victoria. He enters.*

INT. LOBBY. NIGHT

HARRISON *goes towards the lift, gets in. The lift doors close.*

INT. FLAT DOOR. NIGHT

HARRISON *rings the bell.*
STELLA *opens the door, holding cat.*
They look at each other.

HARRISON
Is this convenient?

STELLA
Where have you been?
He does not reply.
Come in.

INT. THE FLAT. NIGHT

She closes the door.

STELLA
I was just sitting – listening to the guns.
He takes off his coat.

HARRISON
Yes, it has been quite a time since we met. I see you've got a cat.

STELLA
No, it belongs to next door. They're not there. It's nervous.

HARRISON
It's a dirty night. Animals don't care for this sort of thing.
They sit.

STELLA

How did you know where to find me?

HARRISON

Oh, I heard you'd moved . . .
Pause.

STELLA

What have you been doing?

HARRISON

Well, I've been out of the country most of the time.

STELLA

You didn't lose your job then?

HARRISON

What, over that affair, you mean? No, no, no, no. I didn't lose my job.
Gunfire. The room shakes.
She stands, moves round the room, looking for the cat. His eyes follow her. She finds the cat, picks it up. She strokes it, her hand trembling.

STELLA

It's so long since we had anything like this. I can't get used to it.

HARRISON

You shouldn't be up here – with all this heavy stuff. You should be in a shelter. You should be down in a shelter.
STELLA *shrugs.*

STELLA

Oh . . .

HARRISON

You're not sorry I came, anyway? Bit of company?

STELLA

I wish you'd come before. A long time ago. There was a time I had so much to say to you. I went on talking to you – in my mind. So I clearly didn't think you were dead. Because you don't talk to the dead, you just listen to what they said, over and over again, and try to piece it together.

Silence.

I missed you. Your dropping out left me with absolutely nothing. Why did you do it?

HARRISON

I was switched. That was the long and the short of it. I was switched.

STELLA

But when? What happened? After all, you killed Robert.

HARRISON

Now, how do you make that out?

STELLA

Oh, you killed him.

Silence.

Why did you send me away that night? That night in the café?

Pause.

HARRISON

It wasn't going to work out.

Bombs. Flares in the sky. The room shakes.

STELLA

But if you hadn't gone away – if you hadn't disappeared – who knows?

Pause.

But now we can say goodbye, can't we? We're not what we were. We're no longer two of three. We're apart.

HARRISON

Goodbye?

STELLA

Yes, we had to meet again to say goodbye. Don't you understand . . . Harrison?

HARRISON

That's the first time you've ever called me anything.

STELLA

I don't know your christian name.

HARRISON

You wouldn't care for it.

STELLA

Why? What is it?

HARRISON

Robert.
Pause.

STELLA

Listen. I think it's over. Don't you? I think the raid's over.
HARRISON *listens, looks at her.*

HARRISON

I'll stay till the All Clear.
They sit in silence.
After a time the All Clear sounds.
They do not move.